For

Ingrid's Husband

With all good
wishes,

Paul Henry.

i.m. Anthony Goble and David Trevorrow

Paul Henry
Ingrid's Husband

seren

Seren is the book imprint of
Poetry Wales Press Ltd.
57 Nolton Street, Bridgend, Wales,CF31 3AE
www.seren-books.com

The right of Paul Henry to be identified as
the author of this work has been asserted in accordance
with the Copyright, Designs and Patents Act, 1988.

ISBN 987-1-85411-438-9

A CIP record for this title is available from the British Library.

The publisher acknowledges the financial assistance of the Welsh Books
Council.

Cover painting: 'Island' by James Donovan (oil, 2005)
courtesy of the Martin Tinney Gallery

Printed in Hoefler by Creative Print & Design, Wales

CONTENTS

It is later one realizes. I forget
the exact year or what we said. But the place
for a lifetime glows with noon ...

Bernard Spencer *(On the Road)*

THREE TREES

for J, J & I

I planted three trees, for privacy
and for feeling near to the soil.
Three ferns, two a fairer shade
of green, the middle one a clone
of my father's dark spire.
(One Spring, he swapped his violin
for a spade.)

    I planted three trees.
Leisurely climbers, I loved them,
suddenly taller when I turned
to look at them again.
Perhaps I planted them too close.
The wind blows in from the sea
and they seem to conspire
against me.

    I planted three trees.
It snows. Sand hurries
through the kitchen's hourglass.
I am nearer the soil
than ever I intended to be.
Above me

    three, fern-haired men
point to the cold stars,
all is silence, but for a spade
played out of key.

THE SNOW DOME

First sun, then snow ... my father floats up the lane
in white jeans, a white rose in his claw.
He cuts a Lear-like figure, drifting alone
through the sun and snow.

Wherever your mother goes, I follow
he mutters, brushing the icing from her stone,
its doorstep to a colder house. It snows

and shines about the ornamental scene.
We can't see for the petals of the rose.
He says she kissed his bald head in the lane,
first with sun, then snow.

DUETS

The night my mother died I followed
my father's car into the night.

The lights on that loneliest of roads
like an order of monks, heads bowed,
lit only their drizzled habits.

Their prayers fizzled out into darkness,
led nowhere except to her silence,
the bungalow where we shared a room,

my father and I, who had not spoken
for ten years, let alone sung
a duet together, of howls

in identical pyjamas, in twin beds.

*

My father composes himself
at the Steinway, presses *PLAY*

on the tape machine
and waits for her first note ...

(Handel's *V'adoro, pupille*
which, by good fortune

she sang unaccompanied
in F Major, for visitors,

one bright afternoon
in 1974.)

GESTURES

I could, of course,
walk to your house
and die on its step.

Warm from your bed,
mistaking my rattling
teeth for the milk

you'd open the door
in pink slippers
and find me lying there

with one eye open.

*

I spy ...   the last star
to disappear
through a giant curler in your hair.

*

In your absence
which is the rest of my life
and unlike Archimedes

who calculated the earth's mass
in grains of sand

I will devote my sentence
to counting the minutes
as they fall

through the hourglass of your days.

*

The cat idles on my chest.
I hold your letter up to the sky.

How to decipher
your feline *y*'s, crucified *t*'s
open-topped *a*'s and *o*'s?

The cloudy watermark
becomes a woman's face.

*

I want you close before I go.
I want you in the fire's glow
then outside in the graveyard's dirt.

I want you where the tide is low
and the sea's lips barely part
for breath to say "I told you so."

I want you close before I go.

*

I've made you my password.
Your name lets me in each day,
your name and your age.

Absurd, how these plastic keys
diminish you, stay silent
when your name is played

and how easily, without knowing,
you let me in each day.

*

Once I whispered in your ear
in the shrubbery of a summer.
Remember?

I even bought you a ring.
That was something.
Can you hear me singing

at the kiss-gate still,
at the sea wall?
Did we meet at all?

*

Here's something cold for you –
the intelligence of water.
(I should like to see you shiver.)

Lay down in its equation.
It will soon work you out,
intricately at first, then harder

lifting your back from the bed
so you're half-fish, half-woman.

Years after you've surfaced
shivering, golden, I'll be here,
student of the river

the cold pool where you lay.

*

It must have happened years ago,
this light between us, this hurt.
I want you close before I go.

*

In the fire's glow,
in the graveyard's dirt,
where the tide is low ...

*

Who will console this room
now that you've come and gone?

The wind in the chimney?
The smouldering grate?

The last star
in its universe burns

then disappears.

OCTOBER

The sun lurched back and fore
all the way down to the shore.

Facing out the rain and sea
the doll's house pastels seemed to say

Once you were fair, now you are grey
while we have stayed this way.

Untied, the wrong dog flew
after another dog's shadow.

Come back, damn you! he called,
feeling the wind's chill.

THE VIEWING

In the tiled hall
her horned bust of Venus
keeps its style

for all the lovers' beads
about its smile.

*

Here's her portrait.
I've seen its double
in those sixties thrillers,
sandy paperbacks she's kept
in the loo, for their titles:

The Snow Was Black
by Georges Simenon;
Léo Malet's *Micmac Moche
au Boul' Mich'*; Ed McBain's
Lady, Lady, I Did It!

Or, *Walk Softly, Witch*
by Carter Brown
whose smitten private eye,
drawn to its *femme fatale's*
"magnetic" legs,

compares himself to
an iron filing.

*

I suspect her life
had known such heights
as the model
in the Blunenfeld poster
on her bedroom wall,
who might

　　　　　　or might not
let go of the Eiffel Tower,
who is poised between flight and fall,
her dress an opened fan.

I'll quit tomorrow
her ashtray says.

　　　　　　　*

A fridge magnet's
History of Art –
from da Vinci to Warhol,
nine doodled faces,
Van Gogh's without an ear,
Dali's a squeezed balloon –
lies in the dog's bowl.

Did she burn her lip
on this Twin Towers cup?

　　　　　　　*

Outside, her bicycle
leans, tilted, just so.

Cobwebs tie it to the tree
in case a thief should call.

BETWEEN TWO BRIDGES

...See, now they vanish,
The faces and places, with the self which, as it could, loved them,
To become renewed, transfigured, in another pattern.

T.S. Eliot (*Little Gidding*)

8pm

Wind scales the river in its mud.
It squirms and pirouettes to the tide's score –
dance of a reptile, forging its cast in silt.

Here comes a friendly stray, with marble eyes.
And here, someone's ditched a fridge. Boats
ghost-boats, Anon's boarded-up work

wait beyond plank and oil drum jetties
for names to be painted back – *Angela* ...
Dragonfly ... *Pride of Newport* ... *Norma's Ark* ...

I look for her name. (It brought me here
from clearer water, twenty years upstream.)
A swan drifts down to a castle's ruin.

A train crosses. On board's my teenage ghost.
"Tonight," he mimes, "I'll walk these streets with you.
I'll break my journey here. We'll walk all night

then one of us will stay and one take flight."

Redundant steel poles form a queue.
Their heads sprout dead sprigs, buds
whose clenched fists shake at the blue sky,

its sails drifting, too easily, out to sea.

11pm

I meet him inside a symmetrical park,
where Edwardians, in ghostly whites
swing massive pendulums

and the moon rolls through football goals.

I meet him where they can't touch us –
the bridge limpers, the black eyes,
the vet bills for three-legged dogs

the piss emporiums, the furnaces,
the palest faces to miss
the last train home.

I meet him inside a symmetrical park.
We touch fingers, touch trees,
kick through shallow leaves

through Hornbeam, Sallow Willow,
Maidenhair, Flowering Ash ...

The smoky heads on glass pillows,
the limpers from east to west
in time for the last bus

they can't touch us.

2am

I follow his stagger up Stow Hill.
Taxi lights transfigure him,
draped in plastic road signs:

chevrons, white arrows
on blue shields – King Cone.

The wind beats its head on stone,
on glass, on Linda Barker's smile.

Perhaps he has walked from hell
and perhaps I am dreaming him
but I follow him, past lock-ups

where a hell's angel's dream,
in pieces, is shown the light.

I follow him over the motorway.

Tracks, pylons, scrapyards ...
the town's raw nerves
twinkle, a child's dream

lulled in the moon's headlamp.

I follow him under a railway bridge,
its thin, wire whine of breaks
or is it the wind's harmonica?

Between two bridges I follow him

past a wave sculpted in steel,
a boat they found inside the mud
and thought an ark to save the port ...

The same current underfoot
drags us on. I can't keep up.

I catch the breath of those who drowned
to keep afloat this listing town,
the steel hull of it.

Only the wind raises them
and a few words perhaps, a name

cut in marble or wood.
(I am not too drunk to salute them.)

The bank runs out. He sheds his cape.
A smudged lamp erases him.

The cradle under the big bridge
is a pendulum, marking time.
It ferries its load, back and fore ...

The river shuffles on to the sea.

5am

The river's nightshift nears its end, slips through an arch of daylight.
Cranes, their loads still, have caught nothing but stars all night.

The first train. His face in mine and, mirrored, a half-raised hand.
He should smile. Soon he'll be walking greener banks with his friends,
setting nightlines, building fires, though I shan't envy him

except when he's drinking it dry and, walking in this later time,
I notice the river, barely a slough of itself in the cracked mud –
as if the moon had taken a long straw to the years and sucked.

He pulls away. The wind puts its lips to an arcade.
A seagull on a barber's pole waits to open its blades.

8am

Wind scales the river in its mud.
It squirms and pirouettes to the tide's score –
dance of a reptile, forging its cast in silt.

Here comes the stray with marble eyes.
He seems to belong here. I watch him
chase and bark the river on its way.

And here, someone's ditched a red armchair.
Prifardd of mud, I lounge in it.
A train crosses. A swan sails near.

Downstream, the cradle ferries its load
back and fore, back and fore ...
as town and river rise from their beds.

Like parts of a clock the small boats
and their jetties rise. I look for her name,
the woman who brought me here. If I wait

I might drift, between two bridges, in my chair
like *Angela ... Dragonfly ... Pride of Newport ...*
Norma's Ark ... I might find her.

Note. *"Prifardd": tr. "Chief Bard" – upon whom a chair is bestowed at eisteddfodau.*

WEATHERVANE

I live and die by such turns,
last blacksmith in a steel town.

The wind blows me north

and my silhouette thins
to a fine stalk

        disappears.
I have shoed a stable of ghosts.

The wind blows me east

and you catch my right arm
raised in anger.

        (Rain and rust
may yet bring it down.)

I live and die by such turns.
Repeat, after me:

        Unlucky!
Down in the mouth!

The wind blows me south.

Who was it nailed me
to the wind's cross?

I will need a steel heart
to survive another winter.

I will need a steel fist.

The wind blows me west.

I live and die by such turns –

north   east   south

now west again.

                 I have learned
how the sea moulds itself
on its anvil

               high tide ...
low tide ...

              By such turns
I live and die, hammering

an eternity ring
on a whim's mandrel

knowing what once weighed true
becomes lighter than air

a fairground from a forge.

The wind blows me north.

I live and die by such turns.

SIX MEN IN SEARCH OF A CAR

They have left their desks in mid sentence,
come out into the early rush hour
to push a car that isn't there.

They have turned a corner, in unison,
a makeshift pack, crew, squadron
because this is what men do well

on a field, at sea, in the air ...

But there is nothing to put muscle into,
no war, no coalface

only this space, and redundancy
in the faces of six men

as if the lift they descended in
had suddenly jolted between floors.
Where's the bloody car?

Steel melts in their arms. They turn

and lean towards a light breeze,
to disparate spaces in offices
filled with women's voices.

THREE WOMEN RUNNING FOR A BUS

Not a race but three women running
after their shadows, away from the sun
along a city pavement – my wife
my mother, my daughter – at 9am.
I'm on the top deck, waving at them.
It is as if the road were a treadmill,
a case of running and standing still
but my daughter's a metre in front
and my gasping mother has lost
a peach from her bag, it rolls
into the path of a cyclist.
My wife cries *Wait! Halt! Stop!*
with a traffic policewoman's arm
and I'm calling back like a fish
miming its life's soliloquy

but they can't hear for the glass
which will rain onto their heads.
The driver pulls away from the kerb.
Just look at their desperate faces
like a red bus was all they had loved.

INGRID'S HUSBAND

The roadside leaves leapt out
as if to flag me down.

I stopped for some razor-blades.
The shop assistant asked
Are you Ingrid's husband?

No. But afterwards,
all the dwindling miles,
I wondered what she was like,

Ingrid, what soap she used,
if her hair was the colour
of these crazy leaves

and if she was mad or sane
or some shade in between.

Perhaps if we met
I'd grow to love her name.

I have seen leaves migrate
to parallel lives –

blown through an underpass
from the eastern side
of a motorway to the west.

Perhaps I should have answered *Yes*.

LETTERS

Tired from crossing two oceans
your father's war letters
lap against the porch.

Your mother lets them in,
waves and waves of them,
sweeps them through the house
and out to the coal bunker.

If he dies in Burma,
if the paper bag he shoots
on guard duty shoots back
you are not born

        and *Dearest All* ...
begins the tide, over and over.

BILL OF LADING: TO THE 'ONE LIFE' FREIGHT COMPANY

after Eugenijus Alisanka

Keep him out of the rain.
It crowds his mind, short-circuits
the heart and brain.

Tell him the sea's hills
are the towers of Vilnius.
Collect what tears spill.

For the journey's leg by rail
put him by the window
or else, with the mail.

When he tries, let him talk.
If his crate rocks or splits
stand back, let him walk.

For the long night's flight
give him a child's chair,
his wife's laughter, moonlight.

Do not assume he hasn't thought
them through as much as you,
the laws of company freight.

And please do not confuse
the journey with how it is
travelled. His is no cruise.

Do not deliver his crate
(what's left of it) on time,
to some grey, industrial estate.

But let the damaged goods decay
with pebbles, bladderwrack ...
lost properties of a bay.

MID MORFUDD

Allow me to translate myself,
the wind through bare branches.
I knock about this tiny house
with a mirror held up to my face.
I was blessed with two tongues,
a cariad in the north
and a lover in the south.
Both wear red waistcoats
that drip like blood about them
in the breeze of twin farmyards.
And both cut me in half
when we make love. Is it they
or I who got displaced?
I leave them to their different songs,
their beds, their half-dug trenches –
one spade travelling north
the other south – half thrilled
and half filled with dread
at this vision I have
of them knocking through soil
to meet, like escapees
completing the same tunnel.

THE SKYLIGHT

Somewhere our belonging particles
Believe in us. If we could only find them.

W.S. Graham *(Implements in Their Places.)*

It's summer outside this winter house
with its fire in every room.
Two seagulls cross the skylight.
Yesterday it was snow-dust
they picked through, instead of sand
and the waves chose not to break.

The same light, in the long break
of '69, visited this house.
We'd had our swim and the sand
stuck to us. We sat in this room,
said nothing, watched the dust
drift on its current of light,
had little in common but that light
which would see fit to break
throughout our lives, stirring old dust.

Each wave of sunlight then, in this house,
carries the two of us in that room,
carries our dust, our grains of sand.

*

Shaping a fish out of sand
you made it a race against the light,
the sea, the crowds ... there was no room.
Build and break, build and break ...
I followed you up to the house.
Our wet prints dissolved to dust
in the narrow lane.

Here, moondust.
I touched your palm, the dusty sand
felt precious.

            Back inside the house
we played cards under the skylight,
I waited for the silence to break.

                    *

I have waited in so many rooms,
particles of this spinning room.
I have lived inside the dust
of wanting you, afraid to break
like the fish you shaped out of sand.

                    *

Two seagulls cross the skylight.
It's summer outside our winter house.
There is room for a ghost or two on the sand.

                    *

That's you, that's me ... dust in the sunlight.
We swim and break and drift about this house.

THE WHITE BALLOON

In a dark arcade
there is only this white balloon

and the echoes of my steps
trying to keep up with it

always a meter ahead
on its current of air.

A square of light grows
in the distance.

I break into a run.
The balloon picks up its pace

swerves off course
when I try to kick it.

Once I was a child
on a wide beach

chasing a big ball
the wind had stolen.

Breathless now,
in a dark arcade

my heart echoes after
a white balloon.

THE BLACK GUITAR

Clearing out ten years from a wardrobe
I opened its lid and saw *Joe*
written twice in its dust, in a child's hand,
then a squiggled seagull or two.

                                   Joe, Joe
a man's tears are worth nothing,
but a child's name in the dust, or in the sand
of a darkening beach, that's a life's work.

I touched two strings, to hear how much
two lives can slip out of tune

                                 then I left it,
brought down the night on it, for fear, Joe
of hearing your unbroken voice, or the sea
if I played it.

THE SHOESHINE'S DAUGHTER

There are coat pegs on the alley wall
above the shoeshine's pitch.

The sun buffs his bald patch,
the down on his girl's arm.

In full swell, the older women
fall silent at her laughter

as tired rivers remember
the springs from which they came.

Sole wears out cobble,
cobble wears out sole.

It's always been this way.
Ask the shoeshine.

The breeze takes a leafy branch
and buffs a window pane.

A cloud hangs its cloak on the wall.
The shoeshine's daughter laughs again.

Lisbon

FIVE NOTES FROM ST RÉMY

I

Is it the only note the wind knows –
this orange beachball on a pool?
It makes no sound, no tune.
Inside, a Satie nocturne
waits, forever, on the piano.

II

Can you hear?
Three fields away, someone
is learning the musical saw
in A. Listen ...
Is it the only note they know?

III

A hammock creaks from a lime.
Francoise wears it like a toga,
trails an arm in leafy shallows.
Is it the only note she knows?
I decorate her hair with a rose.

IV

A bookish dog, disturbed
by lavender in the key of A
(is it?) lifts up his head
from Dali's *Journal d'un Genie*
as if, as if to say

V

Borne across the sky
on a white tray a cicada
ends its *Fugue for Beard and Saw*
with the only note it knows –
a drop, before a downpour.

THE LION GIRL

A small girl, on the safe side of the glass
presses her palm to the lion's paw and blows
into his face through a narrow slat
where two reinforced panes almost meet.
The lion shakes its head again and roars.
The little girl laughs. A crowd gathers.
Her father stands beside her, films the scene
from behind another screen. Almost insane
the lion paces upstage then down to the child
who will always be four on her father's hand-held
recording, except that the sun plays on the pane
and moves her onto the other side, so the lion
passes through her encased reflection
as she touches both sides of the glass, a mane
for her hair, the lion's face in hers.
She laughs again and, shaking her head, roars
out of the lion, out of herself as the lion.
But for the glass she would eat the strange man
with a camera in his face, she would spring
and the crowd would scatter about him, screaming.
She would make a red rag of her father, lying there,
his camera in pieces, his wide stare
fixed on the evil sun. What comes between
a lie and the truth is merely a glass screen.
The girl drags a paw across her mouth,
her bright red lips. She bares her teeth
instinctively, then drags her limp prey
by the arm, towards the exit of the zoo.

SUMMER READING

Bernard Spencer and Disneyland don't mix
but a book entitled *With Luck Lasting*'s a must
to get me through the week.

                              Titania,
our cloned chalet, stinks. Radios blare:
a World Service tribute to 'The King',
Prague and Dresden, bailing out their floods,
the two missing girls ....

                         On small verandas,
to keep off the sun, the red, white and yellow
Miko flower turns on its stalk.
Those obsessed with roundabouts and food
grow fat beneath it, smile

                              while too high
to see, beyond 'the nothing of the air'
a hawk tunes its dial.

IS THERE ANYBODY THERE?

For being so gullible
he kept it from them –

how he'd pushed the Ouija glass
and spelt out *Llanfair P.G.*

in full, and smirked
when 'Wil y Glo' repeated

go-go-go-goch.

The only one in the family
not to believe in ghosts

he kept it from them until
walking through a familiar wall

one night, on his way to the prom
he noticed four chairs at a table

with just the glass left to hold.

NEW YEAR'S ECLOGUE

Somewhere on this planet

> Awash with sirens, our town
> drinks in the new year.

he's wearing my scarf

> The soft incisions of her speech
> were a low tide, marking time.

and if it smells at all of me

> It's the same world we ghost through
> but she more quickly than I.

against his red, red nose

> A conga will come to my door
> if I wait for long enough.

he'll never tell me

> Her flowerpots, tune them in.
> I'll play her name to the wind.

I'll never know

THE WAITING ROOM

An empty coatstand in a public building, in August.
Even this is draped with your absence.
The rags of a seagull's cry hang from it now.

Nothing is devoid of love.
How many years did I waste, listening out
for your voice?

              The park through a window,
swollen with leaves, smothers its coatstands well.

Thin veils of clouds, a city's prayers,
fall away to the west. For a split second
I can see your eyes.

              But if I break my gaze
the gull has slipped its hook, the sea
is a long way away.

THE STOOGE

The café at Orcombe Point
vanished like a magician's prop
from its stone plinth.

Laughter from the sky.

Here's where he sat,
staring, sip after sip,
easily taken in by the tide.

Applause from the strand.

Dark handkerchiefs.
An occasional white gull
shaken up to the clouds.

Lone heckler.

The radio played Acker Bilk's
Stranger on the Shore.
The waitress wore a pinafore.

Red flag, white flag ...

From east to west the sun
waved its bright wand
across his stupid face.

A curtain of rain.

Did he not hear
the sea's knuckles click
before he disappeared?

Smoke. Music.

THE SHELL HOUSE

Press your ear to it.
You can almost hear the tide.
What year is it?

I'll open a window. There
not too wide

                not deafening
but something, a gull
a child's cry

              or this mad ghost
greeting passers by on the prom

Well hello there ... Good to see you ...
Have a

      nice day ...

He has a presidential style.
Perhaps he made you smile.

Loosen that tie.
You're on holiday now.
Sing *My Way* into a cone.

Some days a biplane
drags words across the sky.

Some days it just flies.

There are radios in the pebbles,
small hives, thin swarms
of electric guitars.

High on seaweed
the sandfleas fly.

AND straight in at thirty
it's Thu-hun-derclap Newman!

What crackles the signal?
The sea on the shingle.

Those footsteps are mine.
If I step on a crack, if I
dare ... the flagstones will fly

and all the town's terraces
lift into waves and

was that a wasp or a bicycle?

Press closer ... here's a gull
like a diver
on its board of air.

                  It holds still
then sheds its load onto
someone's auntie's nose.

She powdered it and powdered it
and powdered it and

                  Shit!

Put the shell down. Take six.
Press *Play* on my dream box.
My town was a dreamer's town,
no keep-your-head-down town.

Just wait for that wave to recede ...

I stand on a flagstone, on the prom,
playing myself at chess.
Then sleep, the old master,
pulls up a deck-chair.
'Leave all the moves to me,' he says.
A salty wind blows in from the sea.
I hear groans, and screams.
Knights and pawns stumble
in monochrome across the beach
then fall onto breakers, sharp stones.
They twitch like harpooned fish.
There's a castle, of course,
with gowned rooks for turrets,
and a pier, and a bandstand
where my brother plays a bishop,
my mother 'Queen of The Night.'

They don't make dreams like that any more.
I had a pure mind.
No one had taught me the rules.
Speech was music, music speech.
Only the tide, shifting its pebbles
back and fore, spelled danger.

Check ... check ... check ...
went the water's edge.

Pick up the shell again.

That drum roll's a penny
wished through a crack in the pier.

A puppet laughs, hysterically.

Can you hear the castle choir
rehearsing for Carlo?
Their sycophantic vibratos
swim the wind.

                    Blessem.
Bless the fakers. If you
blessem, the big red mine
by the paddling pool

will not explode

and the blind orphans
in their doll's house

shall be saved.

Breathe in, breathe it in.

Piano scales. Small coughs
in a sunset's vestibule.
What finger is it, on the bell?

And who is plucking the masts?
A harpist has harboured.

Change ears. If you
change ears ...

Hear him? That chime
is our ghost's Chelsea boot
as it kicks the bar

as he bows to Constitution Hill.
He's run the shell house veranda
from south to north

in his Sunday suit.
The tide inches in.

A sky-blue shelter. Inside it
two widows
in plastic bonnets:

I know a man who wears his life
like a too tight Sunday suit,
its waistcoat nailed to his chest
seven times. If I were his wife
I'd ask him to loosen the tie.
He keeps his money neatly pressed
against his heart, like the flower he gave,
once, to a girl, who closed its eye
inside a bible and kept it from the light.

And I know a man who wears his life
like a loose summer jacket,
an inch wider at each shoulder,
a mile longer at the cuffs.
His beard grazes broad lapels
unshorn, unafraid of strangers.
Fluid about him when he laughs
the lining of his soul spills
and shines, in praise of empty pockets.

Pause.

They are staring out to sea.
The wind fills in for a pane of glass.
The shell house is empty.

Where were we? Oh yes.
The tide inching in,
1969

the mad ghost, besuited
with a mackerel's head
gills bellowing

                    for air

the Official Town Ghost
in training for Prince Carlo,
a stand-in for the mayor.

Quiffing the bladder
he turns to rehearse:

*Well hello there ... Good to
see you ... Have a*

                    nice day ...

He has a presidential style.
Did he make you smile?

Loosen that tie.
You're still on holiday.

Sing *My Way* into a cone
before I pull the window to.

Some days a biplane
drags words across the sky.

Some days it just flies.

A TREE FOR DAVID TREVORROW

You painted lean big leaves
and set them in a clear sky.
In our damp flat, in a strange town
they freshened the soft bark of walls.

Big, intricate creatures, they swam
and curled in their element, each scale
and vein refined, over and over.
Meticulous, true to the tree's roots
you believed in God, in blue skies

but also in the craft of a single leaf.

You painted what you saw
and the leaf would find its metaphor.

Sometimes, when the sun was low
and angling dusty beams
in the forest of our living room,
it settled on one of your frames,
turned a leaf into a wing, a sail

or a surfboard, hanging in air
for a spilt-second, above Porthmeor

or something more, the arc of a life ...

You were painting your way home,
following your shoal of leaves.

Home for good now, David
this tree, its private tide, is yours.
It paints itself in your memory
over and over, in praise of blue skies.

Rest easily under its leaves.

A THOUSAND WINDMILLS
FAN HER GRIEF

A thousand windmills fan her grief
and in her palm
a thousand rivers run the leaf.

All the riverbeds they swam
are not yet dry
against the lifelines of her palm.

She glances up. The wind's thief
is in the sky.
It turns the tree and, leaf by leaf

a thousand windmills fan her grief.

LEAF MAN

Leaves, the sky's loose change
glance against the pane.
Look! I am rich in leaves.
I shall step out of this frame
into an October garden
and, staring into the sun,
stuff my jacket with leaves.

Secure in the currency of leaves
I shall not work again
but strut my good fortune
from season to season,
car park to museum,
Winter's "Any change?"
brushed aside with a wave.

All glances are leaves.
I am rich in leaves.
I shall fill each room
of this gallery's mansion
with leaves, and dream
on a bed of leaves,
the next best thing to love.

Leaves, the sky's loose change.
I am rich in leaves.
Staring into the sun
my jacket brims with them.
I shall not work again
but rustle from season
to season, a man of leaves.

OUTSIDE THE GALLERY

The armchairs of octogenarians
sound their horns in the street,

a cot waits patiently at the kerb,
a Bechstein, not looking,
reverses into a Steinway,

a toaster's power station stains
a kettle's cathedral dome,

a china jug conference pours
out of the city hall

past the half-burnt candle
muttering to itself,

the nightclub where mirrors fraternize,
the stadium where hoovers roar
round and round the same track.

It's rush hour. No t.v. stops
to mourn the furry slipper
flattened to pulp by a sofa.

A sudden flock of books
plots its path to the coast

the cliff where two standard lamps
make love, close to the edge

and where the hush of duvets
breaking on shingle will not
go to sleep, go to sleep ...

Further inland, crockery falls
from creaking shelves, its pieces
brushed away by the wind,

curtains lie down, into flowerbeds.

While further in still, on a dusty plain,
herds of unlaid tables wait
for cutlery to rain.

THE YELLOW ROSE

Rides its stalk
on a grey sky,
the wind's rag doll.

Stills for a moment,
bright handkerchief
in a room full of grey suits.

I light a candle in the glass
to keep it company,
the rose that forgot to die.

So often it is
the seemingly frail
who endure.

Now rain tries
to unsaddle it,
this last rose on the planet.

Heavenly Father,
it darkens outside.

Help me to believe
in a yellow rose,

to follow its torch
into the night.

COLLEGE LIBRARY

The book no one else took out
since stamped on 9.10.80
when the Jack Russell froze on its zebra
four stripes ahead of its zimmer
and a wave held back its confession
and a tongue hovered an inch from its cone
and the lifeboat got anchored to its wake
and a finger in the Bay View's window
accused the horizon ... is still here.

He splits it, gently, its shell
back to the light. They take a breath
as swimmers surfacing might.
Their fingertips drift, collide
on lines once whispered by heart.
He snaps it shut again, for good.
The esplanade clock chimes twenty-five ...

Small lines appear at her eyes, which he loves.
His hair comes away in her hand when they kiss.
Someone says *Sh* – a pair of heels on wood
near where the sun falls open at their feet.

TWO VIOLINS

The estate will not be built
for another fifty years.

There is only this mist
a shuffle of wings overhead

and ... listen

               two violins

trying to find each other.

SHED

It was either a mountain or this shed in the rain.
Someone has felted its roof and I'm dry.
Dead spiders hang against the pane,
their legs the broken spokes
of abandoned umbrellas. A web shakes
as heavy thunder rolls down the valley.

I have known worse waiting rooms,
in hospitals, prisons, railway stations ...
A sense of travelling inside the rain,
sustained by flying leaves and the drum
of a thousand fingers, keeps me here.

Two spiders survive. One has crossed
the misted pane to reach the other.

I have known worse places to be lost.

SOLD

Others want this house and soon
we must either leave or stay.
Is it the house or love
we are moving out of?
Perhaps we cannot say

but it hurts, all afternoon
our marriage has moved inside me –
the boys, the prints on the stairs,
the broken down cars, the holidays
in heaven and hell, long Saturdays
in market towns, mad neighbours ...

I pick you a pear from the tree
but you have disappeared again
into that silence you inhabit,
your second home, where a whisper
might fall heavily to the floor –
an incendiary, pear-shaped
and loaded with pain.

Shall we stay or leave then, love?
It's only the years moving inside us
and everything hurts in autumn.
Where shall we put them,
the years, in our new house?
the years we are moving out of?

Acknowledgements

These are due to the editors of the following journals in which some of these poems first appeared: *New Welsh Review, The North, Planet, PN Review, Poetry International Web, Poetry Cornwall, Poetry Review, Poetry Wales, Thumbscrew, The Times Literary Supplement.*

'Between Two Bridges' was originally broadcast on S4C. 'Outside The Gallery' formed part of a longer poem commissioned by Oriel Mostyn and Academi, in response to *The Great Indoors*, a touring exhibition of sculptures by Laura Ford. 'Leaf Man' was written for Lorraine Bewsey's *Poet Portraits* which opened at the Wales Millennium Centre in December, 2006. 'The Waiting Room' was first published in *Answering Back* (Picador; ed. Carol Ann Duffy) and is a response to Patrick Kavanagh's poem, 'The Hospital'.

The musical saw in 'Five Notes from St Rémy' is played by the late Anthony Goble.

I am grateful to Academi for the Published Writer's Bursary which helped in the completion of this collection.

Unreserved thanks to Stephen Knight, for his scrutiny of earlier drafts of this book. For their ongoing support, I am also indebted to Sally Baker, Sheenagh Pugh and Amy Wack.

AUTHOR NOTE

Paul Henry was born in Aberystwyth and came to poetry through song-writing. A popular Creative Writing tutor, he has lectured in this subject at the University of Glamorgan and recently presented the 'Inspired' series of arts programmes for BBC Radio Wales.